IT'S
YOUR
ROOM!

IT'S YOUR ROOM!

A Decorating Guide for Real Kids

Janice Weaver and Frieda Wishinsky

Illustrated by Claudia Dávila

Tundra Books

Published in Canada by Tundra Books,
75 Sherbourne Streeet, 5th Floor, Toronto, Ontario M5A 2P9

Published in the United States by Tundra Books of Northern New York,
P.O. Box 1030, Plattsburgh, New York 12901

Library of Congress Control Number: 2004117247

Library and Archives Canada Cataloguing in Publication

Weaver, Janice

    It's your room : a decorating guide for real kids / Janice Weaver, Frieda Wishinsky ; illustra-
tions by Claudia Dávila.

Includes index.
ISBN 0-88776-711-7

1. Interior decoration – Juvenile literature. I. Wishinsky, Frieda II. Dávila, Claudia III. Title.

NK2115.W42 2005   j747.7'7   C2004-907144-0

ONTARIO ARTS COUNCIL
CONSEIL DES ARTS DE L'ONTARIO

We acknowledge the financial support of the Government of Canada through the Book
Publishing Industry Development Program (BPIDP) and that of the Government of Ontario
through the Ontario Media Development Corporation's Ontario Book Initiative. We further
acknowledge the support of the Canada Council for the Arts and the Ontario Arts Council for
our publishing program.

ISBN 10: 0-88776-711-7
ISBN 13: 978-0-88776-711-1

Design: Terri Nimmo

Printed and bound in Canada

1 2 3 4 5 6   10 09 08 07 06

CONTENTS

BEFORE WE BEGIN

"A journey of a thousand miles begins with a single step."

— ANCIENT CHINESE PROVERB

So you've done it. You've decided that it's time to strip off the fairy-tale wallpaper, paint over the bubblegum pink walls, and make over your room.

Not sure how or where to begin? Then you've come to the right place! This book will help you make sense of all your design dilemmas – from how to choose colors and accessories to how to arrange and organize your space. You'll learn to draw up a floor plan, put together a sample board, and use a color wheel – and have tons of fun doing it all!

But now the hard work begins. Before you ever pick up a paintbrush, you need to settle on the decorating style that's right for you, put together a budget, start to divide your room into zones, and clear the decks of all that *stuff*.

There's no time to waste. Let's get started!

7

First Things First

Before a designer ever puts pen to paper or offers a single suggestion for making over a space, she needs to get to know her client. Good design is all about expressing an individual style, and to do that, a designer must understand her client's likes and dislikes, needs and wants.

Most designers start things off with a client interview, where they'll ask a series of questions. What colors do you like? How will you be using your space? What kind of mood do you want to create? Is there a piece of furniture or a painting you want to build your room around? Is there any design style that really appeals to you?

In your own room, you are both designer and client, but you can still use the idea of the client interview to help you figure out what direction you want your new room to take. Make a list of the colors, textures, and shapes you like best. Think about the things you'll be doing in your room and the feeling you want it to have. Learn about different design styles and decide which ones suit you best. Put together a style file or create a sample board (see sidebar) to help narrow down your choices.

If you really have no idea where to begin, the age of your house and your room's existing design features may give you a starting point. If you're living in an old farmhouse, for example, you may gravitate toward quilts and pine furniture and a country look. A brand-new downtown condo, on the

other hand, may inspire you to go high-tech, with lots of clean lines and industrial materials, such as glass and steel. Even the size and proportions of the room, architectural elements like a fireplace or ceiling moldings, the amount of natural light the room gets, and the direction the window faces can provide you with clues for your new design scheme.

And that's really all there is to it. By thinking about styles and moods and colors and textures, you've started to assess and design your space just the way a pro would. Now it's time to determine how much you can afford to spend.

QUICK TIP

Can't tell rococo from art deco? Not sure where modern leaves off and postmodern begins? If you need some help figuring out which design style is which, flip ahead to the Designer's Dictionary on pages 60–61.

TOOLS OF THE TRADE

The Sample Board

A sample board is a collection of paint chips, fabric swatches, scraps of wallpaper, and photos of furniture and accessories – things that reflect the colors, textures, and moods you want for your room. It's a great way to gather ideas and see how elements you're thinking of using will work together.

To make your own sample board, simply get a thick piece of white cardboard and begin pinning items to it. Look for ideas in magazines or catalogues, on the Internet, and even around your home. Your imagination should be your only limit. Your sample board could include an autumn leaf or a rose petal from the garden, a sheet of Japanese paper, a piece of corrugated cardboard – anything that conjures up the feeling you're trying to create.

Once you've put your board together, live with it in your room for a while and look at it at different times of the day and in different light. Remove pieces that aren't working and add new ones as you find them. When everything seems to go together well, it's time to start shopping!

Building a Budget

The next step of your journey is to create a budget. Now, this may not sound all that exciting, but it needs to be done. A budget will tell you exactly what you can – and *cannot* – afford to do in your space. And if you know what you can afford before you start, you won't be disappointed somewhere down the road.

So how do you make a budget? Well, most people begin with a wish list – an inventory of all the things they would buy for their space if money weren't an issue. To make yours, just jot down everything you would want in the best of all possible worlds. You can dream big, listing a whole room of furniture, a brand-new stereo, and a flat-screen TV. Or you can start small, with a modest can of paint and some new bed linens. Once you have your list, put the items in order of their importance to you. If there's no question that you need a new dresser, that might be the first item on your list. If you included a new desk just because you're tired of your old one, that might come further down the list.

Now it's time to start filling in some rough prices. You can do this by visiting local home-improvement centers and furniture stores, by trawling the secondhand shops, even by flipping through store catalogues that come in the mail. The Internet is also a great resource. Most major furniture stores have websites that list the prices of all the pieces they sell. Sometimes you can even get a discount when you order online.

This can be one of the most fun parts of your room makeover. Take your parents or some friends with you while you comparison shop and dream about all the things you can get for your space. This is also a great time to collect ideas for your sample board and to make additional decisions about what you like and what you don't.

When you have a rough idea of prices for everything on your wish list, take it to your mom or dad and find out what you can actually afford to spend. This part's usually not so much fun. But you've already listed your wishes in order of importance, so it shouldn't be all that tough to cut back

Things always cost more than you bargain for, so be sure to leave extra money in your budget. At least 15 to 20 percent should be set aside for the unexpected.

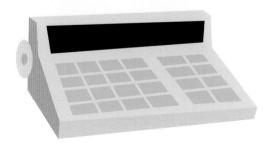

until you're within the budget your parents have set. You may want to enlist their help in this, though. Sometimes it can be hard to tell the difference between what you *need* and what you *want*. Mom will make it clear – pretty quickly – that a new bed is an essential, but a plasma TV is not.

Not so bad, right? Now you have a budget, and you're getting a pretty good idea of what you want to buy. But you're still not quite ready to pry open that paint can. First, you need to take a minute to think about how you're going to tackle any special challenges your room may present.

What If . . . ?

In a perfect world, your room would be big, bright, and all your own, and you could do whatever you wanted to with it. But what if your world isn't quite perfect? There are all kinds of special circumstances you may find yourself grappling with – from cramped space to shared space to space that doesn't meet your physical needs.

What if, for instance, you have to share your room with a brother or sister? In that case, you'll have to find

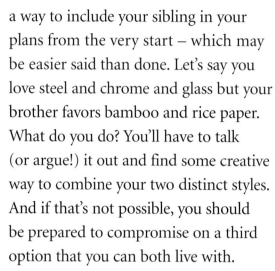

BRIGHT IDEA

Ben says, "My brother and I couldn't agree on how to redo our space, so we literally drew a line down the middle of the room. Now his side is painted blue and covered with snowboarding pictures, and mine is painted green like the left-field wall in Fenway Park!"

a way to include your sibling in your plans from the very start – which may be easier said than done. Let's say you love steel and chrome and glass but your brother favors bamboo and rice paper. What do you do? You'll have to talk (or argue!) it out and find some creative way to combine your two distinct styles. And if that's not possible, you should be prepared to compromise on a third option that you can both live with.

Sometimes there are bigger complications. What if you have problems with allergies, for example? To stop the sneezing and wheezing, you'll probably want to opt for easy-to-clean wood floors and a minimalist style, avoiding the knickknacks and deep-pile carpeting that are every dust bunny's dream. Or what if you or a friend or sibling has mobility issues? Certainly you'll want to leave ample room around your furniture for maneuvering in a wheelchair. You may even need grab bars and wider doorways and furniture that's been modified to make it more accessible. With issues like these, it's important to consult an expert for help.

ZONING OUT

If you're like most kids, the one special challenge you're sure to face is a room that has multiple roles to fill. Usually, your bedroom is more than just the place where you sleep. It's probably also where you do your homework, listen to music, and entertain your friends. It may be where you work on your computer or watch television, and even where you paint, exercise, or practice your tuba.

The key to making multi-purpose rooms work is to divide the space into zones. At a minimum, you will likely need zones for sleeping, schoolwork, and entertaining. Group your furniture so pieces that belong together are actually placed together. Keep your desk and your filing cabinet in one area, for example, but move your entertainment unit and CD cabinet off to another. You can use pieces of furniture, like bookcases or folding screens, to physically divide your space. Or you can create the impression of a divided space by using different paint colors or laying down a variety of area rugs.

Once you have your zones all set up, be diligent about keeping your things in their proper places. Take a few minutes at the end of each day to put your books back on their shelves and your CDs back in their cases (and while you're at it, you may as well stash those dirty clothes in the laundry hamper too). About five minutes a day is all you will need to keep your space looking good and functioning smoothly.

And that's the last of the first steps you'll take on your long journey to a brand-new room. Now it's finally time to roll your up your sleeves and really get to work. So grab some garbage bags and empty boxes and let's start clearing out the chaos!

CLEAR THE DECKS

"Have nothing in your house that you do not know to be useful, or believe to be beautiful."

— WILLIAM MORRIS

Before you start bringing new things in, you first need to clear everything out. Cleaning up and decluttering your space gives you the room to redecorate properly, and helps you take a fresh look at everything you own.

But how do you start clearing out, especially if your room is overflowing with stuff? In a word, *edit*! Evaluate the things you have, keeping what you need and love, passing to someone else what doesn't fit anymore or hasn't been used in ages, and tossing what's broken beyond repair.

But you should know going in that editing can be tough. It's hard to let go of that gnawed old cushion that reminds you of your dog when he was just a puppy, or that rickety chair your aunt gave you when you were little. If you keep only the essentials, however, you'll be starting your makeover with a completely clean slate. That will make it so much easier to create a space that really reflects who you are now.

So put on some music, invite your friends over to help, and get to work!

Making a Plan

When it comes to clearing out your room, having a plan to work from is the essential first step. A plan will help you select your best stuff, pass on what you've outgrown, and toss the junk. It's the only sure-fire way to achieve Total Clutter Clearout (see sidebar).

As part of your plan, decide what you'll do with the clothes, books, toys, and furniture you're giving up. If you know your things are going to a good home, it will be easier to part with them. To find out where and how to donate, contact local community groups or ask the teachers at your school for help. Some organizations offer a free pickup service, which may be useful if you're getting rid of big items, like a desk or your bed. With things you're throwing away, remember not to load up your garbage bags or crates until they're too heavy to lift. And don't forget to check the recycling guidelines and pickup days for your neighborhood.

Your plan should also include ideas on where to store the things you're keeping during repainting. Stuff that's going into a spare room or down into the basement will have to be packed away in carefully labeled boxes. If you're not redoing the whole room, you may be able to get away with moving

BRIGHT IDEA

Robin says, "I invited my friends over for a pile party. Everyone brought clothes, CDs, books and magazines – things that were still good but they just didn't want anymore. We all sifted through each other's piles and took what we wanted, then we gave the rest away to charity."

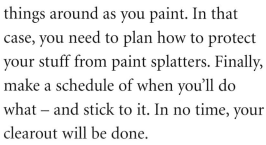

things around as you paint. In that case, you need to plan how to protect your stuff from paint splatters. Finally, make a schedule of when you'll do what – and stick to it. In no time, your clearout will be done.

Your clean and empty room will seem much larger, and it will look, feel, and even sound different. You'll see your room in a whole different way. Take this opportunity to check out where the heat source and electrical sockets are placed. Pull out the pictures you've collected from magazines, look at the decorating ideas you've jotted down and the swatches of fabric you've put aside. Most of all, imagine how much fun it will be to pull it all together and redo *your* room *your* way.

TOTAL CLUTTER CLEAROUT

Clearing out is a great opportunity to see what you own that you really love and what you can happily part with. Just follow these four simple steps to achieve TCC – Total Clutter Clearout.

1. Get three to six boxes, crates, or large garbage bags. Label each one Toss, Give Away, or Keep.

2. Start small, with one drawer or a single shelf. Pick up one item at a time and ask yourself, When did I last use this? Am I keeping it for no good reason? Depending on your answer, place each item in a Toss, Give Away, or Keep container. Give yourself a time limit (like an hour).

3. Take a break, have a snack, talk to your friends, or listen to some music. Then tackle a bigger job, like two drawers, half the closet, or your bookcase. Give yourself another timed deadline (maybe two hours this time).

4. Keep repeating the first three steps until you've achieved TCC. Now have a really big celebration!

COLOR
COMMENTARY

"Color is life."

— Johannes Itten

Okay, you've cleared off, cleaned up, and swept out. You've got your room down to four bare walls, a floor, and a ceiling – a perfect blank canvas. Now it's time to put some color into your life!

The cheapest and easiest way to make a dramatic change in any room is with paint. A few thrilling hours spent in the company of brushes, rollers, and dropcloths will give your room a whole new look. Wait! Did we say *thrilling*? Well, the truth is that painting isn't everyone's idea of fun. It is the critical first step in any room makeover, however. And the good news is that anyone can do it with not much more than care, patience, and some good old-fashioned elbow grease (or the phone number of a reliable professional!).

In fact, getting the paint on the wall is sometimes the easy part. Choosing the right color can be the real challenge. So before you rush off to buy gallons of paint in a shade you'll quickly come to regret, let's learn a little bit about color theory.

19

Understanding Color

Choosing colors will be one of the biggest tasks you'll face in doing over your room. Paint companies offer literally thousands of options, and settling on just one or two may seem next to impossible. All too often, the fear of making the wrong decision scares people into sticking with safe but dull whites and beiges. You don't need to be afraid of color, however. You can narrow down your choices – and ensure you get the look you want – just by learning the basics of how color works and how we relate to it, both emotionally and physically.

Many designers depend on something called a color wheel (see sidebar) to help them select hues that will work well together. The color wheel shows how different colors are related. Those that sit opposite each other on the wheel – like red and green, for example – are called *complementary* colors. *Harmonious* colors are those that sit next to each other on the wheel, like yellow and orange. Designers will often choose a complementary or harmonious color scheme for a space. Or sometimes they will go with a monochromatic look, which makes

QUICK TIP

Be sure to choose the right paint finish. Flat paints hide imperfections in the wall, but they also mark easily and don't clean well. Semigloss paint resists marks and stains, but it reflects more light and emphasizes cracks and uneven spots. Gloss paints should be used only for trim, like doorframes and baseboards.

use of lighter and darker shades of one color.

Before they make their final paint selection, designers also consider things like what direction a room faces and how much sunlight it gets. A room with windows that face east, for example, will get a lot of sun during the early morning, but not much the rest of the day. The best colors for a room like that are those that look good in a lot of artificial light. If the windows face south, the room gets the most sun and the strongest rays. Cool colors like blues and pale greens will help disperse some of the heat. North-facing windows, by contrast, tend to make a space darker and cooler; bright, cheerful colors like reds and yellows can help warm things up in these sometimes chilly spots. Before you make your color choice, think about what direction your room faces and whether you need the lights turned on a lot or a little.

TOOLS OF THE TRADE

THE COLOR WHEEL

The traditional color wheel, developed by an art teacher named Johannes Itten in the mid-1900s, has twelve basic colors. Red, yellow, and blue are known as the primaries; they are pure colors that all others derive from. The secondary colors are orange, green, and violet. They are made by mixing equal amounts of two primary colors (like combining red and blue to get violet). The remaining six colors are called tertiaries. These colors are created by mixing a primary and a neighboring secondary.

You can use a color wheel to understand the relationships between various colors and to narrow down the choices in your own space.

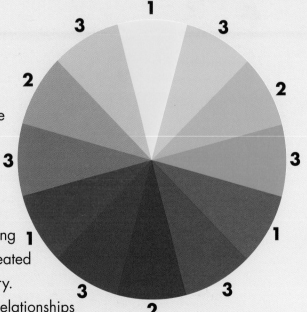

Color in Action

Did you know that the wall color you choose can actually change the size of your room? Well, maybe that's not precisely true, but it can change the way you see the room's dimensions. Some general rules are that pale colors and cool colors, like blues and greens, will make a room look larger, while dark colors and warm colors, like reds

QUICK TIP

You can choose colors for your room by looking at things you already have. A favorite T-shirt, a poster you love, or even a CD cover may provide the key to your color scheme.

SPOTLIGHT ON . . . THE BAUHAUS

Johannes Itten, the inventor of the modern color wheel, was part of a 1920s German art and design school called the Bauhaus. The Bauhaus offered courses in everything from painting and sculpture to graphic and industrial design. Teachers at the school stressed basic principles of color and composition, and they encouraged a simple, functional approach to design. Although the school was closed in the early 1930s, its influence can still be felt to this day.

and oranges, will make a room seem smaller. Vertical stripes on the walls and lighter colors on the ceiling can make a room appear taller, while a dark color will lower the ceiling for a cozier feel.

So you'll want to consider how you plan to use your space. Is your room your sanctuary – a restful place to escape the blare of the TV and the squabbling of your siblings? Is it a favorite hangout for your friends? Or is it your creative wellspring, the spot where you work and get inspired? Studies have shown that we often react emotionally – and sometimes even physically – to certain colors (see sidebar). So before you settle on any color scheme, think about what you will do in your room and what kind of mood you want to create there.

THE MEANING OF COLOR

RED: Associated with fire and blood, red makes us feel energized, strong, and loved.

ORANGE: Orange is the color of citrus fruits and autumn leaves. It evokes pleasant feelings of happiness and creativity.

YELLOW: Yellow, the color of sunshine, makes us feel happy and joyful. It supposedly stimulates the mind as well.

GREEN: The colour of plant life, green is a restful hue that suggests freshness and new growth.

BLUE: Blue is the color of the sky and the sea. It creates a cooler, less intense atmosphere, and it makes us feel secure, stable, and calm.

VIOLET: Violet is the color of royalty. It represents power and wealth, and even magic, and it stimulates creativity.

Let's Get

The beauty of paint is that it has a dramatic impact but is easy enough to apply that you can do it yourself (or maybe with a little help from your folks!). What's more, it's cheap enough that it's not a complete disaster if you make a mistake in your color selection or simply change your mind later.

Once you get started painting – and you realize how easy it can be – you may find you don't want to stop at doing all four walls in one basic shade. Try using paint to put a block of bold color on one wall or one section of one wall. Color blocks are a great way to define the zones in rooms that serve more than one purpose, like a bedroom that does double duty as a study area and a friends' favorite hangout (turn

IN THE KNOW

If you want to do it yourself, it helps to get some advice from the pros before you ever pick up a brush. Here are ten insider tips from Mark, the paint expert:

Cover the floor and move as many things out of the room as possible, giving yourself a clear, protected area to work in.	Fill any cracks or holes with a premixed patching compound (available at any hardware store), and then sand those areas, and any other rough spots, smooth.	Tape off the ceiling, base-boards, and other trim with green painter's tape. You'll save time in the long run.	Always cut in (that is, paint the corners and edges with a brush) first and roll (with a paint roller) second.	Roll in one smooth motion from top to bottom (or bottom to top), making sure to overlap the areas you've already cut in.

Started

back to page 13 for more information on creating zones). You can use color blocks to outline the area at the back of your desk, for example, or maybe the section behind a bookcase with an open back. You can even paint a block of bold color behind your bed, as a quick and inexpensive headboard.

If you have a hobby that consumes you or a sport you can't live without, consider getting some letter stencils and painting words that represent your

I WISH I'D KNOWN . . .

"I wish I'd known dark colors were so hard to paint over," says Marco. "When I got tired of the dark blue-black I'd put on my walls, my dad and I had to apply three coats of the new color before the old one stopped showing through."

BRIGHT IDEA

Jessica says, "I got a small can of paint in a darker version of the pale orange I used on my walls. Then I taped off a huge J – for Jessica – and filled it in with the darker color. It's a cool, custom look that all my friends really love."

passion all over one wall. You can fill your room with snowboarding terms, the names of writers you admire, or even some favorite song lyrics.

And just like that, believe it or not, the worst is over! You've cleared out the clutter and there's paint on the walls. You can probably already see a huge difference in the way your room looks. Now it's time – slowly but surely – to put things back together again.

Move the paint tray every now and again so that it's always in front of you and within reach.	Place a large piece of cardboard under the tray for extra protection against spills and drips.	Wrap your brushes and rollers in plastic when you've finished one coat and store them in the refrigerator for use again the next day.	Cover the lid of the paint can with a rag before you tap it back in place with a hammer. This will stop wet paint in the rim from flying out onto the floor.	Give yourself twice as much time as you think you'll need (or three times as much if you are painting windows or other trim).

THREE SIMPLE STEPS

"One's bedroom may be as simple as a convent cell and still have the quality of the personality of its owner."

— ELSIE DE WOLFE

So the paint's dry and your wall color looks perfect. Now it's time to start filling your room with furniture. But hold on a minute! Before you grab Mom (and her checkbook) and take off for the mall, you should spend a bit of time planning and preparing. You need to consider things like how you use your space, how much (or how little) you have to spend, and how many old pieces you need to reuse. Even the shape and size of the room itself can have an impact on the decisions you're about to make.

So how can you cut through the confusion and be sure you're choosing pieces that are practical, attractive, and fit well with your new look? It all starts with some design principles, a floor plan, and a lifestyle review – three simple steps to choosing the furniture that's right for you.

The Fundamentals

There are so many ways to furnish your room that you probably don't know where to begin. You have to think about styles, needs, colors, shapes, and of course, price. It's easy to get overwhelmed by all the questions that have to be answered. Should you reuse what you have or start fresh with new? What kinds of fabrics and materials should you choose? How strict do you want to be in applying your design style to the furniture you pick? How much furniture is too much, and how much is too little?

Just as it helped you to know a little color theory before you chose your paint colors, it will also help you to understand a few simple design principles before you head for the furniture store. Most decorators use these guidelines to help them decide how to mix and match fabric patterns, how to weigh form against function, and how to create rooms that are well balanced and pleasing to the eye.

When it comes to bedroom furniture, you'll probably just need to cover the basics – a bed, of course; a dresser or an armoire to store your clothes; maybe a desk for doing homework; and somewhere to sit and relax. Whether you're buying new or making do with what you already have, functionality should be your first concern. Above all else, you need a bed that's comfortable, a dresser that has room for all your clothes, and a desk that's the right height. Now is not the time to be too dazzled by appearances. That high-tech steel chair may look great, but it's absolutely useless if it makes your back ache after two minutes of sitting.

Of course, you can't forget about your design scheme when you're choosing new furniture. After all, that country-themed room just cries out for a wicker armchair and a white-painted iron bed, while a Japanese bedroom will never look right without a futon that sits low to the ground. The best pieces will be both attractive and practical – what designers like to call a perfect marriage of form and function.

This is also when you want to start thinking about fabric. From your bed linens to your upholstery, you need to make decisions about patterns, textures, and colors. A good starting point is to choose a large-scale pattern for your biggest piece of furniture – like a duvet cover in an oversized floral print – and to go with smaller-scale fabrics for smaller pieces. It's fine to mix and match. Even stripes and florals can be used together if they share the same basic colors. You may want to limit yourself to only three patterns when you're just starting out, but don't be afraid to experiment until you find a look you like. Get out your sample board (see page 9) to help narrow down your choices.

With furniture, as with everything else in your room, you should go ahead and break the rules if that's what feels right to you. There's nothing that says you can't pair a weather-beaten old desk with a sleek modern chair. You're creating a space to live in, after all, not a stage set for your friends and family to admire.

QUICK TIP

The materials that your furniture's made of will have a huge impact on the look and feel of your space. Wood adds warmth to a room, while industrial materials like glass and iron and steel are colder but have cleaner lines.

Furniture That Fits

Before you start shopping for furniture, you first need to look with a designer's eye at your actual physical space. Is your room large, small, wide, or narrow? Does it have high ceilings or low ones? How many windows does it have? Where are they, and which direction do they face? Is it the closet big or small? Or are you missing a closet altogether?

BRIGHT IDEA

"I got frustrated trying to draw all my bedroom furniture to scale for my floor plan," says Simon, "so I went on-line and downloaded a kit for free. It included graph paper and cutouts for beds, chairs, desks, and dressers in all the standard sizes."

QUICK TIP

When you're planning furniture placement, don't forget to consider the space you need to move around your room between the pieces. You don't want to have to squeeze into or climb over your bed every day.

Your physical space can give you a lot of clues about which furniture to pick. A huge bedroom probably calls for bigger pieces, like a chunky wooden sleigh bed with a substantial headboard, while more modest spaces usually look better with pieces that are smaller in scale, like a desk with delicate tapered legs. When you're buying new, you need to choose pieces that work with your room's existing proportions. A big room with too little furniture will feel cavernous, while a small room that's packed to the rafters can seem like a cluttered mess.

A floor plan (see sidebar) is a great way to experiment with different arrangements until you figure out exactly how much furniture your room can comfortably fit. It's no fun lugging that heavy oak desk around – scratching your floors and scuffing your new paint job – until you decide where it should go. And it's even less fun to find out the hard way that the new dresser you bought won't fit through your bedroom door.

TOOLS OF THE TRADE

THE FLOOR PLAN

A floor plan – a to-scale drawing of your room – lets you try different furniture arrangements before you actually start moving things around. There's nothing worse than finding out that your bed is too long for the wall *after* you've hauled it across the room.

To make a floor plan, get a sharp pencil and some graph paper. Pick a scale – one square on paper might represent one foot, or maybe twenty-five centimeters. Measure the length of each wall carefully and transfer the measurements to the paper. Measure and mark the doorways, noting which way the door opens. Then add windows, closets, electrical outlets, phone jacks, radiators, fireplaces, built-in shelves – anything in your room that can't be moved.

Using the same scale, make paper cutouts of the furniture you're planning to keep. Now you can try every imaginable arrangement without so much as lifting a chair. If your bed has always been flush against the wall, try angling it for a brand-new look. That antique dresser half-hidden by the door might look great against the main wall with a poster of your favorite movie star above it. Use your imagination – and enlist the help of a friend, who may see your things with a fresh eye.

When you shop for furniture, take your floor plan and a measuring tape with you. Will that big armoire block your doorway? Can you move your bed somewhere else so that great desk fits beside the window? Your little paper floor plan can save you a lot of headaches – and more than a little disappointment.

Let's Start Shopping

Okay, now you have some basic design principles to draw on and a floor plan to steer you in the right direction. It's finally time to go shopping!

When you hit the stores, don't forget to keep your lifestyle in mind. Do you have lots of oversized sports equipment you have to store or big trophies to display? If so, those things may be a factor in your furniture selection. Maybe you need a sturdy armless chair for playing the guitar or a wheeled bed that can be pushed out of the way when it's time to practice your dance routines. If you sketch or paint, you'll probably want a flat, easy-to-clean work surface and somewhere to store all your supplies. And if you're sharing your space with a sibling or a non-human companion (see sidebar), you may want to invest in folding screens or other pieces that will help you get some solitude when you need it.

This is also the time think again about ways of organizing your space to keep your mountains of belongings under control. Fresh paint and new furniture are great, but they won't have much impact if they can't even be seen through all your piles of junk. Flip back to page 13 to remind yourself how zones can help create a room that will serve all your needs. The flip ahead to the chapter on storage for some concrete ideas on reining in your closet and your desk area.

IN THE KNOW

When it comes time to choose new pieces for your bedroom, some advice from the pros can help you avoid making costly mistakes. Here are five essential tips from our furniture expert, Marian:

Make sure that any furniture you buy will fit into your room, as well as through doorways and up stairwells.

Choose pieces that aren't too trendy. Trends come and go, but classic, well-built furniture is always in fashion.

Stick with the same family of colors. If you have a dark mahogany desk, choose other pieces in dark woods with red undertones to complement it.

Look for furniture that can be changed as your needs change, like a storage unit that can be added to later.

Think of ways to reuse and recycle pieces you already have. New knobs can give a second life to an old dresser.

FINDING SPACE FOR FIDO

Don't forget about man's best friend when you're planning out your new space. If you have a pet who thinks he's your roommate, you'll have to take him into account. All animals need a comfortable place to sleep and access to drinking water, even if they're fed somewhere else in the house. And with every pet – sad to say – noise and odor are problems that will need to be addressed.

Some pets come with their own special challenges. Gerbils and other small caged animals, for example, are nocturnal and like to use their wheels at night. If you don't want to be kept awake, you should try to place the cage as far away from your bed as possible.

A fish tank – with all its pumps and filters – can also be quite noisy. And a filled tank will be very, very heavy. You'll need to get a really sturdy stand for it, and you'll want to be sure you place it where there's no chance of knocking it over.

If your roommate is a cat or a dog, pet hair will probably be your biggest problem. Consider investing in removable slipcovers that can be stripped off the furniture and washed when they get dirty or are covered in fur. Area rugs that can be tossed in the washing machine are also a smart choice. These also work well if you have an older pet who sometimes has accidents or a younger one who hasn't been housebroken yet.

Finally, if your furry little friend believes that your bed is also his, you may want to think twice before you spend all your savings on that immaculate white linen duvet cover that shows every single speck of dirt. For all your furnishings, opt for darker colors or busy patterns that will hide the grime.

LET THERE BE LIGHT

"Space and light and order. Those are the things that men need just as much as they need bread or a place to sleep."

— LE CORBUSIER

Many professional designers say that the easiest way to dramatically transform a room is with paint and new lighting.

Yet most people just screw a bare bulb into an overhead fixture in the middle of the room and think they're done. They don't always realize that proper lighting is critical to the appearance, mood, and usefulness of a room – especially one that's filling multiple roles, like a bedroom that's also a study area and an entertainment headquarters.

So how can you use light to its best advantage in your own special space? Read on to find out!

Lighting Lowdown

It's true that no room makeover is complete without a lighting plan. But making one isn't as complicated as it sounds. You simply need to decide how you'll be using your space and define what type of lighting you'll need.

Just what does that mean? Well, in general, lighting falls into one of three categories: ambient, task, or accent. *Ambient light* is the most basic form. It usually comes from a wall- or ceiling-mounted fixture, and it basically replaces sunlight at night and in rooms that don't get enough direct outside light. *Task lighting* is used to make specific tasks – like reading or putting on makeup – easier. Task lights, such as table and desk lamps, give a direct, concentrated beam of light. Finally, *accent lights* add drama to a room by highlighting paintings, plants, pieces of sculpture, and so on. They are a purely decorative type of lighting.

So when you're sorting out the lighting plan for your bedroom, you start by listing all of the ways your room will be used. Is it only for sleeping? Then maybe you can just stick with ambient lighting, like one ceiling-mounted fixture. Planning to read in

bed? Then you'll need some task lighting, like a lamp on your nightstand or a wall-mounted fixture that you can pull out over the bed. Is your bedroom also where you do homework and work on your computer? If so, you'll need task lighting on your desk.

What about accent lighting? Do you have some photographs you really love? What about a hobby you can show off on the wall, like a shelf full of snowboarding trophies? If there are things in your room that you'd really like to draw attention to, ask your parents about installing a track light with fixtures that can be moved around until

I WISH I'D KNOWN

"I wish I'd known to choose a nightstand big enough to hold a reading lamp, as well as my alarm clock and a glass of water," says Janine. "Whenever I read in bed, I have to get up and turn off the overhead light when I'm done."

they're in just the right position.

You can probably see now why it's so important to think about how many lights you'll need – and of what type – before you call in the electrician or go rushing off to your local lighting store or home-improvement center.

⦿ TOOLS OF THE TRADE ⦿

TRACK LIGHTING

Track lights are the most flexible type of lighting system. Fixtures can be moved to any position along the track and then rotated and aimed wherever they're needed. Track lights are also an excellent choice for highlighting objects hung on a wall. It's important to position them properly, however, to reduce or eliminate shadows and reflections. Use the chart below as a guideline:

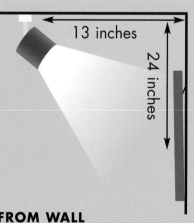

13 inches

24 inches

DISTANCE FROM CEILING	DISTANCE FROM WALL
24 inches (60 cm)	13 inches (33 cm)
36 inches (90 cm)	20 inches (51 cm)
48 inches (120 cm)	26 inches (66 cm)
60 inches (150 cm)	33 inches (84 cm)

Bulb Basics

Believe it or not, your lighting job is only partway finished once you've chosen your fixtures. Next, you have to decide what kind of bulbs you're going to use. That may seem like a minor detail, but in fact the quality of light your fixtures provide can vary dramatically depending on your bulb choice.

There are several different types of bulbs. The most common are incandescent bulbs (yup, those are the ones invented by Thomas Edison). Many people prefer these because they are familiar and inexpensive to buy, and they give off a warm, yellowish light. But incandescent bulbs also radiate a huge amount of heat, which is wasteful and makes them expensive to use.

Compact fluorescent bulbs are a popular alternative. These bulbs can be used in regular fixtures, but they do cast a cooler, bluer light than we're used to. Compact fluorescents also cost much more to buy than incandescent bulbs. But the good news is that they last five to ten times longer and require much less energy to operate. Since lighting accounts for as much as 15 percent of the electricity used in a home, that makes them more economical in the long run. The sidebar on the next page shows what you should look for whenever you're shopping for bulbs.

So now that you know the best ways to illuminate your space, let's start thinking about all the fun and fanciful things those lights can show off.

The sidebar on the next page shows what you should look for whenever you're shopping for bulbs.

IN THE KNOW

Before you invest your time and money in a lighting overhaul, check out these insider tips from our lighting pro, Ken:

Try before you buy. Many lighting stores will let you take lamps home to test out in your space before you purchase them.

Use dimmer switches to control the amount of light a fixture gives off. They can even be installed with table lamps.

Go with versatile track lights and portable floor and table lamps rather than fixed lighting. That way, you can move your lights around if you redecorate your space later on.

Set your track lights so they hit the items they are highlighting at about a thirty-degree angle. This will help reduce glare and shadows.

Choose compact fluorescent bulbs for a cooler light and greater energy efficiency.

WHAT DO ALL THOSE NUMBERS MEAN?

Have you ever taken a close look at a light-bulb box? If you have, you've probably noticed a bunch of numbers running up the side or across the bottom. These numbers tell you how energy-efficient the bulbs are. To determine a bulb's efficiency, called *efficacy* by lighting experts, divide the lumens by the watts. The higher the number of lumens per watt, the more efficient the bulb is. If you keep that simple formula in mind, you'll always be wattage-wise.

LUMENS

This is the amount of light a bulb produces. Lumens are also sometimes called *light output.*

WATTS

This is the amount of energy the bulb consumes. Sometimes the wattage is listed as *energy used.*

VOLTS

This is the charge of electricity needed to make the bulb work. Most bulbs require 120 volts, the standard voltage available at home outlets. If you choose a higher voltage, your overall efficiency will decrease.

HOURS

This is tells you how long the bulb should last. It's also often called *bulb life.*

THE WELL-DRESSED ROOM

"Great things are not done by impulse, but by a series of small things brought together."

– VINCENT VAN GOGH

Well done! You're making great progress. You've got rid of the junk, put paint on the walls, sorted out what furniture you need, and thrown some light on it all. The rest is easy – sort of.

Your next step is to start dressing the room. Yes, you read that right – your room does need to get dressed. Just as you may feel an outfit isn't complete until you've added the perfect belt or a pair of dangly earrings, your room isn't ready to go without art on the walls and coverings on the windows.

Dressing your room does signal that you're nearing the end of your makeover project, but it's no less important a step than choosing the paint or placing the furniture. And best of all, it's a great way to start putting your own unique stamp on your space.

Art Can Be Anything

You don't have to own an expensive painting by a famous artist to enrich your life with art. The key is to zero in on what you love and what you like to do now. Look for posters or pictures in magazines that match your interests. Take photos of your friends and paste them together in a huge collage. Once again, your imagination should be your only limit. You can hang your wall with a T-shirt from a concert you loved or a brightly colored kimono you treasure. Art can be anything!

Before you rush off and grab that hammer, though, you first need to think about how to hang your art so it will look its best and not damage your walls. Framing posters and pictures helps them stand out and be noticed. But how do you make a number of different items look as if they belong together? You could frame them all with identical mats (the border between the frame and the art). Or you could put them all in similar frames – all in metal or wood, or all the same color or shape. If custom framing is not in your budget, check out all the inexpensive, ready-made frames you can buy or look into getting your posters professionally mounted on stiff-backed boards.

I WISH I'D KNOWN

"I wish I'd known enough to use the right kind of plugs and hooks to hang my pictures," says Ben. "When I used regular hooks on the brick wall in my room, they didn't hold. One of the pictures fell down, and the glass and frame cracked."

When you have all your pieces framed or mounted the way you want, it's time to start figuring out how you'll hang them. The first step is to lay the pieces out on the floor. Think about how to balance the way they look. You can use symmetry, where one side of the group mirrors the other – like hanging two big posters by the same artist on either side of your dresser, for example. Or you can use asymmetry – balancing a big poster on one side of the dresser, for instance, with several small photos on the other. This is a little funkier and less formal.

Whether it's one piece or a grouping, art looks great above furniture. But designers will tell you that your artwork shouldn't be wider than the furniture below it. Leave eight or ten inches (20 to 25 cm) between the top of the furniture and the bottom of the art, and about two inches (5 cm) between each of the pieces.

When you like the way you've arranged the art on the floor, it's time to move up to the wall. Hanging art takes more than one person, though, so enlist a good helper to hold things and to make sure you're getting everything straight and at the right height. Start with the central piece first, positioning it so the middle of the picture is just above your eye level. (You may be heading for a growth spurt!) Then add the other pieces around it, using the measurements you came up with on the floor. Keep going until you've got everything straight, even, and exactly in place. And just like that, your walls are all dressed and ready to go.

BRIGHT IDEA

"Instead of hanging pictures of myself and all my friends on the walls," says Cara, "I put some on an open shelf and others on my windowsill. Now I can rotate pictures when I feel like I want a change. And I didn't have to worry about making holes in the wall."

Window Dressing

Now let's talk about window coverings. Although windows are meant to let in daylight and the great outdoors, you don't want your life put on public display, and you don't want to be exposed to winter drafts or summer heat waves.

But what kind of covering should you choose? Store catalogues are full of options: track-mounted drapes, tie-back curtains, sheers. There are shutters, solid or louvered. There are blinds of paper, cloth, or bamboo. There are blinds with metal or plastic slats, and even ones that rise from the bottom windowsill, instead of rolling down from the top.

BRIGHT IDEA

"I love my view of the sky," says Nicole, "but the window looked too empty and boring. So I asked Dad to put up a plant hanger. Now I have blue sky with a leafy green plant framed in the middle."

I WISH I'D KNOWN . . .

"It was fun shopping for blinds, but I wish I'd known to take a sample of my paint color with me," says Karyn. "I couldn't remember the exact color and had to go back to the store later to exchange what I'd bought."

The most important thing to know about windows is that you shouldn't cover what doesn't need covering. If you have a well-insulated window that looks out on the gorgeous branches of a pine tree, you may not have to cover it at all. Or if the top view is fine but the bottom is boring (or vice versa), just cover the part that needs it.

And that's really all there is to the well-dressed room. Believe it or not, we're almost there! There are just a few more final things to do before you're finished.

A BRIEF WINDOW SURVEY

If you do decide to cover your window, ask yourself these questions first:

1. What direction does the window face? If it faces east, the early-morning sun may interrupt your sleep. If it faces south or west, you may need to block the heat of the afternoon sun.

2. What's outside? If your room faces a big backyard, you're not likely to be bothered by noise and lights. But if you face a busy street (or a sports stadium!), you may need heavy drapes or blinds to block out what's going on outside.

3. What region do you live in? In an area with distinct seasons, your needs may vary through the year. Heavy drapes may be right for one season, but you may want to replace them with light curtains at other times.

4. What colors already dominate the room? If they're bright colors, give your eyes a rest with quiet tones of beige or off-white on the windows. If the walls are muted and you crave just one splash of, say, lime green, maybe your window dressing is the place for it.

LET'S GET ORGANIZED

"A place for everything, and everything in its place."

— SEVENTEENTH-CENTURY PROVERB

Okay, your new space is looking pretty cool. But let's face it: any room that has to serve multiple purposes is going to be packed to the rafters with *stuff*. It's impossible to get rid of it all, so you have to figure out how to keep it from spiraling out of control. The best way to do that is to store anything you don't need to get at every day and organize anything you do.

The good news is that well-planned storage and organizing solutions will pay big dividends in the end. In an organized space, you'll find it easier to locate the things you need, easier to keep everything clean (so Mom will be happy), and easier to show off all the work you've already put into making over your room.

Say Yes to Storage

HELP!
It looks like a bomb went off in my room, and I can never find anything I need. But how can I get organized without erasing all the personality from my space?

Jesse, 14

Organized people get a bad rap. They are seen as uptight control freaks, while the disorganized are considered wacky and creative. In fact, a lot of people are afraid that if they try to get organized, they will lose that certain something that makes them unique. Nothing could be further from the truth. A good organizing system can be just as creative as you are, and with all the time you save by being organized, you'll be able to focus on the fun stuff that really makes you *you*.

So by now, you have your room divided into zones – the desk area for

QUICK TIP

Make sure your favorite things are the most accessible. Most people use the same 20 percent of possessions (or wear the same 20 percent of clothes) over and over and over again.

IN THE KNOW

Getting organized – and staying that way – is easier than you think. Check out these insider tips from Shelley, a professional organizer, to help get you started:

Look up for storage space. Fill unused wall space with shelves, hooks, bookcases, and tall furniture.	Assign a home to everything you own. Clothes and papers and other things left lying around create the impression of clutter.	Be merciless when it comes time for a clearout. Toss out duplicates of things you already own and stuff you're keeping just for sentimental reasons.	Pick double-duty furniture. A bed with drawers underneath can provide tons of extra storage space.	Use existing furniture in creative new ways. Clear out the bottom draw ers of your dresse and use them to store CDs, DVDs or papers.

Photos

studying, the bed for sleeping, the stereo and maybe (if you're lucky) an entertainment system. But these zones all come with their own storage and organizational . . . um, shall we say challenges? A stereo is great, but what are you going to do with those hundreds of CDs you've collected? A work area is a necessity, but with it come books and papers and pens and pencils – all of which need to be kept in some kind of order.

The simple truth is that your bedroom probably has to hold all your worldly goods – every stitch of clothing, every textbook, every piece of technology you've ever owned or trophy you've ever won. But don't despair! The sidebar below proves that there are some quick tricks for getting a handle on all that stuff. And once you've got the basics down, we'll take a look at how to tackle two of the worst trouble spots – the closet and the desk area.

Invest in practical, attractive storage bins. You'll be more likely to put things away if you have an efficient, easy-to-use system in place.

Make the most of wasted space, like the area under your bed or on the back of your bedroom door.

Plan a reward for yourself for successfully tackling an organizing job. This will make the task more enjoyable – and help you see it through to the end.

Be realistic about how much time you'll need. If you think a job will take half an hour and it takes four, you'll probably give up partway through.

Resolve to spend a few minutes of every day cleaning up and putting things away. This will save you oodles of time in the long run.

Closet Chaos

Without question, the closet clearout is the most dreaded of all organizing jobs. Most people find it impossible to be ruthless when it comes to their clothes. They tell themselves that old shirts will come back into fashion, that small sweaters will miraculously fit again, and that pants with broken zippers or rips in the knees will somehow mend themselves. Once you commit to clearing out and organizing your closet space, however, you'll be glad you did. Things you have forgotten you own will reappear like a phoenix rising from the ashes. You may even discover that your wardrobe is twice as big as you thought it was!

QUICK TIP

If you're sharing your room with a slobby sibling, invest in a screen to divide your space and block the mess from view.

Now, we know what you're saying: "Cleaning out my closet is *so* boring!" That may be true, but fortunately there are some very simple things you can do to keep this black hole of your bedroom more orderly (see sidebar). And the good news is that if you invest a little time upfront, you'll get it back ten times over. We promise!

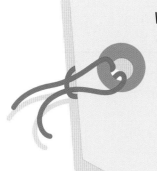

A LOT FOR A LITTLE

If you and your sibling share a bedroom with just one overstuffed closet and can never tell whose clothes are whose, buy some inexpensive plastic hangers in two different colors. Put all of your clothes on hangers of one color and all of your sibling's on hangers of another color. Now when you open the door, you'll be able to see at a glance which clothes are yours!

TIPS FOR THE CLOSET CLUTTERERS

Is your closet bulging at the seams? Do clothes go in and never come back out again? Here are some quick ideas that will help keep your closet under control:

1. Put off-season clothes in a chest or in a storage bin that can be rolled away under the bed. That will free up room in your closet and make it easier to find the things you need.

2. Group your clothes so that longer items (like dresses and coats, for instance) hang at one end and shorter items (like shirts and blouses) hang at the other. You may find you now have space below the shorter items for a shoe rack or your hockey bag.

3. Add a second clothing rod to double your storage space. This can go behind the existing rod if your closet is deep or under it if your closet is tall.

4. Install extra shelves to give you additional space for folded garments, like sweaters, and for storage containers. Make sure all your containers are clearly and accurately labeled so you can find things when you need them!

5. Take no prisoners when it comes to deciding what will stay and what will go. Anything that you haven't worn in eighteen months or that doesn't fit you anymore should be donated to someone who can use it.

Desk Disorder

If you always find yourself crouched over your books on your bed instead of working at your desk a few feet away, it may be because your work surface is so cluttered you've forgotten it's there. That's hardly surprising, given the hundreds of pieces of paper you acquire over the course of an average school year – everything from

SPOTLIGHT ON . . . FRANK LLOYD WRIGHT

Frank Lloyd Wright (1867–1959) was perhaps America's best-known architect. During the Depression years of the 1930s, he began designing Usonian houses, small, affordable homes made with inexpensive building materials. To make the most of the limited space in these homes, Wright also designed most of the furniture for them, as well as numerous built-in storage units. These built-ins also helped reinforce the houses, which were usually made with simple plywood walls.

handouts and assignments to essays that have been graded and returned. And that's not even to mention all the books, CDs, software programs, magazines, and other odds and ends that seem to migrate to the desktop like birds flying south for the winter. But don't despair! With just a few quick space-saving and organizing tricks (see sidebar), you can dig out your desk area and conquer that clutter.

Ta-da! Now you've got a cool space that's freshly painted, newly decorated, and completely clutter-free. It may be hard to believe, but there's just one more step left in your room makeover.

TIPS FOR THE DESK DISORGANIZERS

Has your desk disappeared under a mountain of junk? Do you want to clean it up but don't know where to begin? Check out these useful tips for getting your work surface in order:

1. Install a shelf above your desk (get someone to help with this!) to hold reference books, computer software, even a bookshelf stereo. This will clear off the desktop and give you more room to work.

2. Buy file folders in a variety of colors and designate one for each school subject – blue for math, green for English, and so on. Then be diligent about keeping your assignments and essays filed away.

3. Get an inexpensive stand and move your CPU under the desk. You can even invest in a printer stand with drawers for storing paper, printer cartridges, pens and paper clips, and so much more.

4. Mount a big calendar on the wall in front of your desk. It will be easy to see at a glance what assignments are due and when.

5. Resolve to make your desk area only for homework. Find another place to store your CDs, old magazines, and pictures of your friends.

PIZZA PIZZA PIZZA

FINISHING TOUCHES

"To thine own self be true."

— WILLIAM SHAKESPEARE

You're almost there. All you need now are some final accessories, those last few pieces that will make your room look just perfect.

Sounds simple, right? Not so fast! Accessories come in literally thousands of different colors, patterns, shapes, and sizes. They can be just about anything – from pillows and vases to screens, lamps, and area rugs. It's an embarrassment of riches. But with so many great options to choose from, you may feel that it's impossible to figure out what you need.

Don't panic! Remember your trusty sample board? It's time to pull it out once more and review the colors and textures of your room, and the mood you've tried to create there. With that and some helpful tips from a pro, you should find it a breeze to accessorize your space.

Let's Say It with

We all rely on accessories to tell the world who we are. Chunky beaded earrings, a belt with a big silver buckle, a watch with a Pittsburgh Penguins logo on it – all say something about the things we like or the way we see ourselves. It's no different when it comes to accessories for your bedroom. Those are just another way to communicate your interests and give your space that personal touch.

When you're choosing accessories, the first lesson to learn is that you

QUICK TIP

Don't forget to use mirrors to accessorize. They expand space and can be beautiful on their own. Be sure they reflect something attractive, though, like other accessories or a piece of framed artwork – not your dirty laundry!

IN THE KNOW

Accessories can really spice up your space, but sometimes it's hard to know which will work and which will not. Here are some tips from Aileen, an interior design consultant, to help you narrow down your choices:

Think about the mood you want. A vase filled with long grasses will give a "Zen" feel to an Asian-themed room.	Choose items that reflect your interests. If you've visited exotic places, frame maps or foreign money and hang this "travel art" on your wall.	Try for the unexpected. Use objects like twigs, pine cones, rocks, or seashells to bring the outdoors in.	Be selective. Even if you've collected a hundred hats, you may want to display only a few at any one time.	Choose pieces of varied sizes but link them by color or shape. A group of red candles – some fat, some thin – can make a nice display.

Accessories

don't need many to make a strong statement. Old-fashioned? A collection of pressed flowers in carved frames from the flea market will express your romantic side. More of a country type? Use an old cream pitcher to house your rulers and pens. Is modern your look? The gunmetal box you keep your CDs in gives that message loud and clear. Just as a jazzy belt can transform some ho-hum jeans and a T-shirt, accessories can make even the most practical, bare-necessities room look fantastic.

Don't rush out and try to find all your accessories at once, though. Part of the fun of accessorizing comes from collecting pieces over time. Gather them around you slowly – and don't get discouraged if it takes time to find just the right objects. The pieces that end up meaning the most to you – like the seashells you collect during your summer holiday – will probably be the ones that evoke happy memories. But you've got to make those memories first!

A LOT FOR A LITTLE

If you can't afford, or don't want, expensive accessories, look around at what you own already. Decorate your space with jewelry, pictures from magazines, concert tickets – anything you feel like. Visit yard or garage sales or ask your family for unused items that you can recycle as accessories. Sometimes all it takes is a little elbow grease to bring a dusty old model car to life or a touch of polish to revive a brass figurine.

Mix and Match

A well-designed space is more than just a feast for the eyes – it's a treat for all your senses. After all, what's better than flopping down on a bed covered with soft, fluffy pillows or stepping into a room full of fresh-cut flowers? Choosing accessories that

QUICK TIP

Use texture to create contrast and visual excitement in your space. If all your surfaces look the same, your room will lack interest.

SPOTLIGHT on ... SISTER PARISH

Dorothy May "Sister" Parish (1910–1994) was a famous American interior designer who liked to mix styles and patterns to create a whimsical and comfortable environment. She disdained trends and felt the key to good design was to have things look pleasing to the eye. She wrote, "I have never developed a look or followed a trend because I knew that every person's life differs from every other, and everyone's needs are therefore different."

appeal to each one of your senses will make your room look sensational, feel wonderful, and smell delightful.

Try using texture, for example, to heighten your senses of sight and touch. Silks and satins will give your room a luxurious, elegant feel, while the rough, knobby textures of bamboo and wicker will create a more rustic mood. For a modern look, sleek and shiny is the way to go. Try decking out your room with a highly lacquered jewelry box or a tall silver vase.

Don't forget about your sense of smell! Why not infuse your space with the sweet aromas of vanilla, lavender, or roses through potpourri or with fresh flowers? Flowers are a delight for the eye, too, especially when they're set

BRIGHT IDEA

Marnie says, "I bought about twenty cheap, plain pillows and painted a different word on each one in bright fabric paint. Then I scattered them all over my room. My friends and I like to mix and match them to make funny sayings, song lyrics, or pillow poems."

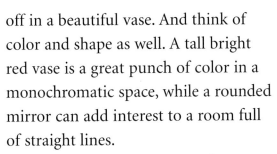

off in a beautiful vase. And think of color and shape as well. A tall bright red vase is a great punch of color in a monochromatic space, while a rounded mirror can add interest to a room full of straight lines.

Bravo! You've cleared the clutter, painted, furnished, organized, and picked the perfect artwork and accessories. All your work has paid off, and your room is finished. You've created a space that reflects your style, taste, and personality. Now it's time to put up your feet, turn on the music, and relax and enjoy it.

PILLOW TALK

Pillows aren't just for sleeping anymore. They're great for lounging, too, and can bring an unexpected burst of color into your space. Get some round or triangular pillows to introduce a few unusual shapes. Use pillows with fake fur or animal prints to inject humor and charm. Oversized, overstuffed pillows can make great extra seating, and you can change them around in summer and winter to create a seasonal look.

If you're feeling really ambitious, make a cozy pillow nook where you can read, listen to music, or gossip with your friends. Surround the nook with sheer drapes hung on a rod to close it off from the rest of your space and really get some privacy. Add a small rug and – presto! – you've got a room within a room.

Designer's Dictionary

ART DECO: Often associated with the Jazz Age of the 1920s, Art Deco design is characterized by smooth lines, geometric shapes like triangles and circles, and industrial materials such as plastic and chrome. Bold, dynamic colors – reds, greens, and golds – are the palette, and products of the machine age, including cars, planes, and ships, are the inspiration.

ARTS AND CRAFTS:

This style is built around the Arts and Crafts movement, which emerged in the early 1900s as a reaction to the Industrial Revolution. It celebrates hand-crafted pieces over machine-made products. Wood furniture, moldings, and accent pieces are featured, as are rich paint colors like deep browns, greens, and coppers.

ASIAN: Rooms designed around an Asian, or Japanese, theme are quiet and calming. They use natural materials such as bamboo and stone, and colors that evoke the great outdoors, especially browns and greens. Furniture is low to the ground and kept to a minimum, and these rooms are always clutter-free. Textures are introduced through rice-paper accessories or grass wallpapers.

CONTEMPORARY:

Contemporary rooms feature neutral color schemes (browns, creams, whites) and clean, smooth lines. Pale woods and modern materials like glass and steel are standard. Pillows, rugs, or artwork are sometimes used to introduce a splash of bold color.

COTTAGE: This is a relaxed, comfortable style that uses the soft blues, greens, yellows, and beiges of the seaside for its color palette. Designers often pair floral fabrics with stripes and checks, and bring in texture with wicker furniture, baskets, and natural fibers. Iron furniture and metal or ceramic accent pieces that look as if they've been left outside to weather a few storms are also common.

COUNTRY:

A country room is built around time-worn pine or painted furniture. Fabrics in checks, florals, and stripes are typical, as are handmade accessories such as wooden bowls or toys and clay vases. Sometimes designers will use items like old milk jugs or cookie jars in the shape of barnyard animals to inject a bit of fun into these informal, easy-going spaces.

ECLECTIC:

Eclectic design brings together a variety of styles and historical periods. In a eclectic bedroom, for example, designers may pair a modern, streamlined bed with Art Deco travel posters and a vintage alarm clock from the 1930s. The key to eclectic design is to contrast styles, textures, and finishes, but also to use color or the lines of the pieces to link them together.

ENGLISH COUNTRY:

English country is slightly more formal than standard country design. It features floral fabrics, chintz, and fancy tassels and trim. The color palette is based on the soft blues, greens, and pinks of an English garden. Framed prints of plants and flowers often adorn papered or stenciled walls.

MEDITERRANEAN:

This style uses strong, bright blues, whites, and yellows to evoke the countries bordering the Mediterranean Sea, especially Greece, Italy, and southern France. Textured plaster walls and tiled floors are often featured, and plants and flowers help to bring the outside in.

MODERN:

This clean, stream-lined style is characterized by smooth surfaces, strong lines, and a lack of ornamentation. Black, white, and gray are the colors of the stark modernist palette, and industrial materials like steel, glass, and concrete are its building blocks.

SOUTHWESTERN:

A southwestern room is built around the colors of Arizona, New Mexico, and Texas, the states of the American Southwest. It features hand-crafted accessories, warm earthtones, rough textures, and hand-painted tiles. Furniture is most often upholstered in leather or suede and frequently draped with brightly colored woven wool blankets.

Acknowledgments

The authors would like to thank the following people for sharing their ideas, design expertise, and helpful tips:

- Aileen Alvarez of
    Norwalk Furniture
- Painter Mark Bell
- Brenda Borenstein of
    Organized Zone
- Shelley Boylen of
    Bit by Bit Organized
- Joe Ohayon of Art Avenue
- Designer Ettie Shuken
- Patricia Snyder of Drapery Art
- Marian Young of
    Early Canadian Furniture

Thanks are also owed to the staff of
Tundra Books, especially publisher Kathy Lowinger;
editors Gena Gorrell, and Carolyn Jackson; and
designer Terri Nimmo.

Index

JANICE WEAVER is a noted author of nonfiction. Her first two books, *Building America* and *From Head to Toe*, were both named Notable Books by the International Reading Association. *From Head to Toe* was also nominated for a Rocky Mountain Book Award and the Ontario Library Association's Red Maple Award. When she's not writing, Janice likes to agonize over paint colors and flooring options at her Toronto home.

FRIEDA WISHINSKY is the international award-winning author of over thirty trade and educational books. She has been nominated for the Governor General's Award for Children's Literature (Text) and has won the Stockport Book Award and the Sheffield Children's Book Award (both for *Jennifer Jones Won't Leave Me Alone*). Frieda's books have been translated into many languages, including French, Dutch, Danish, Spanish, and Catalan. She lives in Toronto with her husband and family.

CLAUDIA DÁVILA is a yoga-happy, food-loving book designer and illustrator with a passion for recipe-swapping. She has illustrated many books, including *Art for the Heart* and *The Girls' Spa Book*. Born in Chile, Claudia now lives in Toronto with her husband.